Foreword

I0484421

When a child is the victim of abuse or neglect, it is the responsibility of each member of the child protective service and criminal justice communities to provide a timely and appropriate response.

To promote the coordination and teamwork needed to ensure such a response—and to minimize additional trauma to children—a growing number of jurisdictions have established multidisciplinary teams (MDT's) comprising professionals from law enforcement, child protective services, prosecution, medicine, counseling, and related fields.

Forming a Multidisciplinary Team To Investigate Child Abuse delineates the benefits that an MDT offers and provides advice on forming and operating an effective team. Diverse MDT models are described and keys to making the team a success—confidentiality policies, conflict resolution practices, and periodic review—are discussed.

It is my hope that this guide will be a valuable resource to current and potential MDT members and that it will enhance coordination among these professionals and improve the timeliness and effectiveness of their investigations. Only through such improvements can we fulfill our duty to protect children and bring those who abuse and neglect them to justice.

Shay Bilchik
Administrator
Office of Juvenile Justice and
 Delinquency Prevention

November 1998

Second Printing March 2000

NCJ 170020

Two months before her seventh birthday in 1995, Elisa Izquierdo was killed. Over a period of months, she had been physically and emotionally abused, repeatedly violated with a toothbrush and a hairbrush, and finally beaten to death by her mother. Elisa's mother told police that before she smashed Elisa's head against a cement wall, she  made Elisa eat her own feces and used her head to mop the floor. The police told reporters that there was no part of the 6-year-old's body that had not been cut or bruised. Thirty marks initially thought to be cigarette burns turned out to be the imprints of a stone in someone's ring.

An investigation after her death revealed that Elisa had been the subject of at least eight reports of abuse and that several government agencies had investigated the reports. Nonetheless, Elisa Izquierdo was left with her abuser and eventual killer.

Unfortunately, this failure to respond to reports of child abuse in a timely and appropriate manner has happened many times—and is continuing to happen—in probably every State in the country, and almost always for the same reason: As the investigation into Elisa's death revealed, there had been an appalling lack of communication and coordination among the agencies investigating reports of possible abuse. The first recommendation of the New York State commission mandated to find out how to prevent another such tragedy was to adopt legislation to authorize child protection agencies to provide complete information to all members of a county's designated multidisciplinary team (MDT) or child advocacy center.

An MDT is a group of professionals who work together in a coordinated and collaborative manner to ensure an effective response to reports of child abuse and neglect. Members of the team represent the government agencies and private practitioners responsible for investigating crimes against children and protecting and treating children in a particular community. An MDT may focus on investigations; policy issues; treatment of victims, their families, and perpetrators; or a combination of these functions. This Portable Guide deals with the investigative function of MDT's.

The MDT approach promotes well-coordinated child abuse investigations that benefit from the input and attention of many different parties—especially law enforcement, prosecution, and child protective services—to ensure a successful conclusion to the investigation and to minimize additional trauma to the child victim.

Key to the formation of successful investigative MDT's are:

♦ Committed members who have the support of their agencies for the multidisciplinary approach.

♦ An initial meeting during which each member's role and previous experience in investigating child abuse and neglect are respectfully heard.

♦ The development of a mission statement that clearly sets forth the purpose of the team, the scope of its activities, and its guiding principles.

♦ The subsequent creation of a team protocol that specifies the types of cases that will be investigated, the responsibilities of the members, and the procedures for conducting investigations.

Key to the successful operation of an MDT are:

♦ Confidentiality policies that accord with legislative mandates, agency policies, professional practices, and the best interests of the abused children.

♦ Conflict resolution practices that ensure core issues are aired and resolved satisfactorily based on mutual respect and recognition that child abuse investigations are complex, demanding, and frustrating but that they are also important, meaningful, and rewarding.

♦ Periodic self-analysis and outside evaluation of how the team is working so that it continues to achieve the purposes for which it was formed.

Need for a Team Approach

Over the past two decades, the number of reports of child abuse and neglect has greatly increased, straining resources to investigate allegations effectively. A number of cases have been the subject of intense media coverage. Although helping to raise public awareness of the problem, this coverage has also led to a backlash that includes charges of government witch-hunts on the one hand and accusations of government inaction on the other. Whatever the perception, there is significant outside pressure on professionals to act promptly, yet professionally and correctly, when faced with a report of child abuse or neglect.

Research related to child abuse has increased dramatically in the same period. More information than ever before—in the areas of specialized child development issues, victim and offender dynamics, diagnostic imaging, traumatic memory, linguistics, forensic pathology, and others—is available to help practitioners discover the truth of a report. Moreover, to meet the competing demands of child protection, due process, and family preservation, laws have been repeatedly changed and refined in the areas of evidence, procedure, and definitions related to abuse and neglect. The existence of such abundant yet diverse and technical data and legal requirements places significant demands upon professionals who investigate and prosecute these increasingly difficult cases.

No single profession or State agency has the ability to respond adequate ly to any allegation of child maltreatment. Indeed, several professions and State agencies are mandated to report or investigate suspicions of child abuse and neglect or to provide services to abused children or the perpetrators of abuse.

It is now well accepted that the best response to the challenge of child abuse and neglect investigations is the formation of an MDT. In fact, formation of such teams is authorized, and often required, in more than three-quarters of the States and at the Federal level. Hospitals have been using MDT's in a variety of ways for nearly 40 years.

The MDT approach often extends beyond joint investigations and interagency coordination into team decisionmaking. Team investigations require the full participation and collaboration of team members, who share their knowledge, skills, and abilities. Team members remain responsible for fulfilling their own professional roles while learning to take others' roles and responsibilities into consideration.

An effective response to reports of child abuse and neglect is an investigation that is timely and objective and that causes the least possible trauma to children and families. Effective teamwork can prevent further abuse to children and can bring those who harm children to justice. Some of the recognized benefits of a proficient MDT include:

♦ Less ‑system inflicted" trauma to children and families.
♦ Better agency decisions, including more accurate investigations and more appropriate interventions.
♦ More efficient use of limited agency resources.
♦ Better trained, more capable professionals.
♦ More respect in the community and less burnout among child abuse professionals.

These benefits can translate into safer communities.

Types of Multidisciplinary Teams

MDT's can take several forms and may involve different locales:

♦ Some are part of a children's advocacy center (CAC), which provides a child-friendly facility where forensic interviews, and sometimes medical examinations and treatment, are conducted. The CAC may serve as the site for team meetings and trainings and may also house representatives of member agencies. CAC's also often do community outreach and public education. There are more than 400 established and developing centers nationwide.

♦ Other MDT's may not provide the more comprehensive services of a CAC but may establish a particular place for conducting interviews. Such teams may be based in hospitals, prosecutors' offices, or within child protective services agencies. The San Diego Children's Hospital and Health Center has specially trained interviewers who use an area designed specifically for interviewing children.

♦ Hundreds of effective teams are not part of a CAC and do not have special interview facilities. These teams use available resources to accomplish, in different but effective ways, many of the same purposes—reducing trauma to victims and families, improving the accuracy of information obtained during the investigation, and easing the strain on member agencies and investigators.

No single type of team is best. The model you choose will depend on the resources available and the way various agencies function in your community.

Forming a Team

Creating an MDT involves several steps: identifying and recruiting members, developing a mission statement and protocol, establishing and maintaining good working relationships among team members, and evaluating the team's performance.

Some agencies have worked together very well in an informal though systematic manner for a period of time, usually because the individuals representing them work well together. The creation of a formal MDT—by institutionalizing the team and documenting its functions and procedures on paper—ensures continuity of existing coordination and collaboration beyond the tenure of specific individuals.

Team Participants

In many States, the membership of MDT's is defined by statute. Generally, laws authorizing or requiring the formation of investigative MDT's specify that law enforcement, child protection or family services, and prosecution participate. Even if your State does not require such membership, these three disciplines and the medical professions should be considered the core of any investigative MDT. Depending on the resources available in your community, other potential members include mental health professionals, victim services coordinators, court-appointed special advocates, and educators. In federally recognized Indian Country and government reservations, such as a military base, the Federal Bureau of Investigation has investigative jurisdiction and must be included in any MDT.

Everyone on the team must be committed to the concept that a coordinated and collaborative process is required for successful investigation of reported instances of child abuse. That commitment may not be fully developed when the team is first formed, but there must be at least an agreement to implement the team philosophy.

To be viable, an MDT must have support of the leadership of its members' organizations and agencies. To gain support for forming an MDT, seek out professionals working in other MDT's in your area or in your profession and communicate their experience to others in your organization. Share the current literature on the team approach, which overwhelmingly supports the MDT concept. For instance, one study has revealed that in a jurisdiction where an MDT created a close working relationship between law enforcement and child protective services, three out of four cases were referred for criminal prosecution, and nearly 95 percent of those cases resulted in convictions.[1] Those proportions are much higher than in jurisdictions without MDT's. Other research has suggested that MDT's, by reducing the number of investigatory interviews a child must endure, reduce ─system intervention trauma" as well.[2]

Initial Meeting

An initial meeting of potential team members is critical to laying the foundation for success. Any interested person can call, convene, schedule, or coordinate the first meeting. Participants in the initial meeting should discuss their reasons for attending the meeting and the advantages

---

[1]Tjaden PG, Anhalt J, *The Impact of Joint Law Enforcement—Child Protective Services Investigations in Child Maltreatment Cases,* Denver, CO: Center for Policy Research, September 1994.

[2]Henry J, System intervention trauma to child sexual abuse victims following disclosure, *Journal of Interpersonal Violence* 12(4), August 1997.

and disadvantages of implementing the team method of investigating suspected harm to children.

The need for investigations will most likely be universally expressed, sometimes in terms reflecting the frustrations commonly felt by professionals handling these cases. It is important for all participants to hear what other people are saying and to be heard by others. Members will express opinions reflecting their professional training. Their opinions may be heated because they feel defensive about criticism of their agencies or angry about the ways their agencies have failed to protect children from abuse. Statements like the following may set a tone of angry or bitter criticism:

♦ —Too many cases, not enough resources."
♦ —Smeone dropped the ball."
♦ —The facts are too complex."
♦ —The victim's behavior is unpredictable and misunderstood."
♦ —No one understands the restrictions I face."
♦ —You want to put people in jail; I need to put families back together."

It is vital that these comments be understood as the first step in acknowledging the failings of current investigative practice. These are the types of obstacles that face every new MDT.

Because participants generally concur about the importance of the work and need for a team, they should be able to maintain an overall positive attitude. The use of a seasoned facilitator, who will not be a team member, can provide the structure necessary to create a climate of mutual respect and attention. All potential team members should be consulted in the choice of a facilitator, to avoid the appearance of too much control by any one member.

At this initial meeting, participants should also discuss additional team membership—agencies or individuals vital to the proper functioning of the team. Finally, participants should begin to work on a mission statement.

Writing a Mission Statement

A mission statement is a general declaration of purpose—the scope of your team's activities, its goals, and the guiding principles for achieving those goals. It should concisely describe the reason the team was formed and the purpose it will serve. It should be easily understood by team members and by the broader community. Your team should consider the following questions in developing its mission statement:

♦ Why was the team formed?
♦ What are the common values held by each team member?
♦ Who is on the team?
♦ What jurisdiction or community will the team serve?
♦ How does the team want to be perceived?
♦ What types of cases will the team investigate?
♦ What other functions will the team perform?
♦ What challenges does the team face?
♦ How will the team meet those challenges?

Do not attempt to incorporate the answers to all these questions. The mission statement is supposed to be short (five or fewer sentences) and specific enough to provide an adequate measure of success. It should be simple, direct, and inspirational. The preamble to the Constitution, for example, sets forth its mission statement in these few words: —. . in order to form a more perfect union, establish justice, insure domestic tranqu ility, provide for the common defense, promote the general welfare, and secure the blessings of liberty to ourselves and our posterity. . . ." This simple mission statement has guided a very large and complex organization for more than 200 years.

To be relevant, the mission statement must also be tied to the everyday workings of the team's member agencies. Buzzwords, jargon, and platitudes will not provide a clear vision for team members or the community. The mission statement for your team will be the reference point for its protocol, which will be the team's next project.

Writing a Protocol

A properly written protocol is essential if a team is to function well. For an MDT, it is the written understanding of how investigations and other functions will be pursued by team members and the roles and responsibilities of member agencies.

The agencies and individuals signing the document signify their mutual commitment to the team and the team's mission statement.

The team's protocol is a practical, working document. Where the mission statement is conceptual, the protocol is concrete. The protocol serves as a reference when questions or disputes arise within the team. When there is a written agreement specifying investigative roles and responsibilities, conflict is reduced because there is a shared understanding of investigatory practice. Moreover, when investigations are conducted in a relatively predictable and consistent manner, the stress associated with uncertainty is minimized, resulting in less conflict. Diminished interagency conflict means more energy and attention are spent on the investigation itself, contributing to swifter and more precise resolutions. That in turn can alleviate trauma to children and their families.

Because many State statutes now mandate team formation, it is important that you consult applicable State law when drafting your team's protocol. Many teams have also found it helpful to review protocols developed in similar communities. (Samples of protocols are available from the National Network of Children's Advocacy Centers, the four regional CAC's, and the National Center for Prosecution of Child Abuse. See pages 21–23.) However, every community should work out an agreement that suits its own resources and needs. What works in Chicago or San Diego may not work in smaller or more rural communities.

Regardless of the size or location of your community, a number of issues must be addressed in every protocol. As you address these issues, keep in mind the wide range of incidents in child abuse reports—for example, a dirty house, a 2-year-old wandering down a highway, sexual abuse, physical abuse, or suspected child homicide. Balance the need for structure and certainty with the necessity for creativity and flexibility. If you agree in writing to follow a specific procedure, there may be legal or procedural repercussions when that procedure is not followed, no matter how compelling the reason for departing from the protocol. Some teams have used a particularly complex or difficult case as a point of departure when formulating a protocol.

Figure 1 lists questions that will help in creating a protocol. Note that the questions address the —who, what, when, where, and how" of investigations and of team function. In addition to addressing these questions, some teams have found it useful to specify the criteria for arresting suspects, removing children from their homes, and filing charges.

The benefits you derive from your team's protocol will be in direct proportion to the amount of thought, discussion, and analysis of existing practice and challenges that you have invested in developing the protocol.

Dealing With Confidentiality

Confidentiality is often perceived as a barrier to team formation or effective teamwork. Often, this is due to a misunderstanding of the requirements of confidentiality imposed by law. Sometimes, legitimate confidentiality protections are used as an excuse for not sharing information when agencies mistrust each other. Misunderstanding and misuse of confidentiality protections have contributed to the continued abuse and death of too many children. As the commission that investigated the death of Elisa Izquierdo noted, —[The State's] confidentiality laws mandate silence and [its] expungement laws mandate ignorance." Confidentiality laws must continually be reviewed to ensure that their legitimate purposes are being met while, at the same time, allowing information to be appropriately shared.

The first step in determining how your team will handle the confidentiality issue is to look at the governing law. Do not assume that past practice has been or is in conformity with existing law. Federal laws mandating confidentiality have been substantially changed, and States are now permitted latitude to enact laws authorizing investigative agencies to furnish child abuse data to other agencies involved in an investigation. The Child Abuse Prevention and Treatment Act permits dissemination of confidential information to Federal, State, or local government agencies that need this information to carry out their legal responsibilities to protect children from abuse and neglect.

Many States not only permit but require the sharing of such information. Some laws make exceptions to general requirements of confidentiality when data are shared in the

Figure 1

Questions To Help You Create a Protocol

The following points should be addressed in any MDT protocol:

- What is the purpose of the team? This may be the team's mission statement, but it can be more concrete, such as —to investigate all child abuse reports in Box Butte County."

- Who are the members of the team?

- What kinds of cases will the team investigate? All child abuse? Only child sexual exploitation? Only felony physical abuse? Neglect and abandonment ?

- How will investigations be conducted? Who will do what? Who will interview victims and who will interrogate suspects? Who will remove children from their home? Who will collect physical evidence? Who will refer victims for physical examinations?

- When will team members perform certain tasks? Within a specified time from receipt of report? After consultation with other team members? In a particular sequence?

- Where will particular events occur? Will interviews be conducted at a certain location? Interrogations at a different location? Will specific locations be prohibited unless there are unusual circumstances?

- How will team members carry out assignments? Jointly? Who must be present? How long will others wait? Will child interviews be recorded? On video? Audio? Other? Will nonteam personnel be present? Parents or person *in locoparentis?*

- What information can be shared under what circumstances?

- How will decisions be made? By whom and at what stage?

- When and where will the team meet?

- How will meetings be conducted?

- When (or how frequently) will the protocol and team function be evaluated? How and by whom?

context of a team investigation. Teams should remember that most laws prohibit public disclosure only of material gathered during an investigation or revealed in a report of harm. Good professional practice generally requires some disclosure of confidential reports among professionals so that proper decisions can be made.

When information is shared between agencies charged with protecting children and the privacy of individuals, there is arguably no breach of confidentiality. However, sharing information within a team and for team purposes does not justify general or public disclosure of sensitive information. Your team protocol should specify what data will be shared and how and when this can be done.

Keeping the Team Going

A team is like a car in that it consists of multiple parts joined together to accomplish a particular task. In a car, if the steering fails, there is no direction, and if the brakes fail, collisions are unavoidable. Each part or group of parts in a car must be regularly maintained, or the car will cease to operate properly. Likewise, if a team is to continue to function smoothly, the team members must pay attention to maintenance.

Dealing With Conflict

Conflict resolution is one form of preventive maintenance. Conflict that is not properly rectified will cause resentment, retribution, or retaliation. Any or all of those will eventually destroy a team. Unresolved conflict in a team is like rust in a car—it may not be immediately visible, but left unchecked it will deepen and spread, eventually ruining the team. Effective conflict resolution, on the other hand, enhances team spirit, improves team function, and protects the team against failure.

Conflict within a team is inevitable and normal, but team effectiveness is measured not by the amount of conflict but by the manner in which conflict is resolved. Not all conflict is appropriate or necessary. Conflict that thwarts the team's ability to accomplish its mission is *core* conflict and must be resolved in a constructive fashion and by consensus. This does not mean that team members must agree on every point, but they must find ways to support solutions that maintain agency integrity and further the team's purpose. Resolving core conflicts should result in ―win-win" conclusions.

Other conflicts may involve peripheral problems—issues that do not significantly hinder the team's ability to accomplish its mission. Peripheral issues can be dealt with more quickly, without necessarily building consensus. Figure 2 (page 14) lists points to remember for successfully dealing with conflict.

These points can be summarized as follows:

♦ Characterize the problem. Look at it from a systems perspective.
♦ Acknowledge relevant goals and interests by recognizing diverse agency objectives.
♦ Negotiate (but do not confuse negotiation with compromise).

A complete and helpful discussion of these steps can be found in the article by Fargason, Barnes, Schneider, and Galloway (cited in the supplemental reading list), in which the authors note that people involved in the helping professions often try to avoid conflict. Unfortunately, this means that the source of the conflict can undermine long-term cooperation between organizations that serve abused children. When that happens, children, families, and communities are ill served. Team members must recognize the importance of dealing with the real source of conflict in a constructive manner.

Promoting Teamwork

Many teams have found that joint training fosters good teamwork (see figure 3, page 15). Team members who train together may find opportunities to discuss issues of mutual concern, both in the training itself and during social breaks. Spending time together away from the immediate and constant demands of the office provides a break during which the team can focus on its functioning. Moreover, team members hear the same information, which improves shared understanding of the challenges and solutions common during the investigation of reported child abuse. Joint training can clarify understanding of mutual roles and responsibilities.

While not essential, social activities can strengthen team identity and function. Simply combining lunch with a team meeting can serve this social purpose. Some teams sponsor picnics, awards banquets, and other activities to reinforce

Figure 2

Points To Remember When Faced With Conflict

♦ Do not lose sight of the team purpose (see your mission statement).

♦ Look forward to opportunity, not backward to blame.

♦ Be respectful. Ensure each contention is considered. Listen to one another. Be sure each position is understood. Restate the other position in your own words.

♦ Clarify the opposing point of view until you are sure you understand. Find something positive in each view. Avoid defending your point of view until you understand the other.

♦ Do not withhold an opposing point of view.

♦ State your position clearly, firmly, but without excessive emotion.

♦ Once you have been heard, do not continue to restate your position.

♦ Avoid personalizing your position—keep the discussion focused on the issue.

♦ Offer suggestions rather than mere criticism of other points of view.

♦ Remember that conflict within a team is natural and work toward a mutually agreeable resolution.

♦ Base resolutions on consensus, not abdication of responsibility or integrity.

♦ Keep focused on the team's agreed-upon purpose and refer to your protocol for guidance.

the sense of belonging that is vital to effective teamwork. When individuals identify with the team in a positive way, commitment to the team mission is strengthened.

Preventing Burnout

People who work in child protective services, law enforcement, prosecution, medicine, mental health, and other fields associated with children and their families are typically sensitive to the feelings of others. The difficult cases they deal with require an inordinate amount of emotional energy, and tragedy becomes almost the norm of everyday work. They must also face the often unrealistic expectations of the public, the mechanics of the system, heavy caseloads, and inadequate resources. The load can be crushing and can lead to burnout. Burnout is a syndrome of physical and emotional exhaustion, depersonalization, and reduced sense of personal accomplishment. It is a gradual process of loss that can lead to cynicism and ineffectiveness. Recently, burnout has been recognized as a problem not of the individual worker but of the social environment in which people work.

A well-functioning team can reduce some of this emotional loss by providing a much-needed sense of community. When there is a sense of shared values and commitment, there is an accompanying sense that the crushing emotional load associated with child abuse intervention is being shared. Team members can actively encourage one another, understand the stress as others cannot, and work together to find ways of improving working conditions.

Team social activities can also help prevent burnout. While child abuse cases will always be emotionally challenging and

Figure 3

Rules for Effective Teamwork

- Identify a leader.
- Meet regularly.
- Respect others: agree to disagree.
- Listen to one another.
- Be open to constructive criticism.
- Be honest.
- Know respective abilities and limitations.
- Understand respective roles and responsibilities.

draining, they will be less so for a team than for a practitioner working alone.

Evaluation

Periodic evaluation is essential if the team is to know whether it is functioning effectively and being properly maintained. One method of evaluating team function and maintenance is to get regular feedback from team members. Members must be honestly but constructively critical of the team's performance if the team is to survive and thrive. This self-analysis can take place at regular meetings, during specially scheduled meetings, or even during a team retreat designed expressly for evaluation and renewal of purpose. A questionnaire can be prepared and submitted if team members sense a need for anonymity.

Although this self-analysis is important, there is always a danger that the team will not view itself objectively. Evaluation of the team by victims, their families, outside agencies, members of the general community, and agency managers or supervisors is critical to proper team development and as a matter of attention to constituents. The team should develop a method of regularly soliciting, collecting, and analyzing input from these sources. This process need not be elaborate or expensive. What is important is that the team see itself as others see it. If others see a need for change in a particular area, the team should give serious consideration to the suggestion without, however, subordinating its mission to public opinion or public pressure.

Conclusion

It is beyond the power of government to prevent this from being a world in which children suffer and die, but it is the responsibility of government to protect children and bring those responsible for mistreating them to justice.

Secrets That Can Kill: Child Abuse Investigations in New York State
New York State Temporary Commission of
Investigation, 1996

If the thousands of professionals who have had the good fortune to be part of a successful MDT could contribute to this guide, they would likely say the team approach has made an immense difference in their communities and in their ability to do their jobs. They would relate first hand how the team improved the quality of child abuse and neglect investigations through enhanced communication and cooperation among its members. They would say that by pursuing a multidisciplinary team approach, they also reduced the number of interviews child victims faced and the length of the investigative process and intervention, thereby preventing further trauma to these children.

The MDT method of investigation significantly improves the response to child abuse. Forming and maintaining an investigative MDT will not be easy. At times during the process, people may be discouraged. It will perhaps seem easier to continue doing things —the old way" than to expend the effort to create an effective team. However, practice and experience clearly demonstrate that children and their families, communities, and the professionals serving them benefit greatly from the existence of an appropriately functioning MDT. The best mechanism to ensure that government fulfills its obligations to protect children and bring to justice those responsible for mistreating them is the cooperation, coordination, and collaboration of the responsible agencies in an investigative MDT.

Author

Mark Ells, J.D.
Research Assistant Professor
University of Nebraska–Lincoln
Center on Children, Families and
the Law
121 South 13th Street, Suite 302
Lincoln, NE 68588–0227
402–472–3479
402–472–8412 (fax)
E-mail: mells@unlinfo.unl.edu

Supplemental Reading

Alexander RC. To team or not to team: Approaches to child abuse. *Journal of Child Sexual Abuse* 2:95–97, 1993.

American Prosecutors Research Institute, National Center for Prosecution of Child Abuse. *Investigation and Prosecution of Child Abuse*. 3d ed. Alexand ria, VA: National Center for Prosecution of Child Abuse, 1994.

Baglow L J. A multidimensional model for treatment of child abuse: A framework for cooperation. *Child Abuse & Neglect* 14:387–395, 1990.

Besharov D J. *Combating Child Abuse: Guidelines for Cooperation between Law Enforcement and Child Protective Services.* Washington, DC: American Enterprise Institute for Public Policy Research, 1990.

Bross DC et al. (eds). *The New Child Protection Team Handbook.* New York, NY: Garland Publishing Co., 1988.

California State Department of Justice, Office of the Attorney General. *Child Victim Witness Investigative Pilot Project: Research and Evaluation Final Report*. Sacramento, CA: Office of the Attorney General, June 1994.

Dinsmore J. *Joint Investigations of Child Abuse: Report of a Symposium.* Washington, DC: U.S. Department of Justice, Office of Justice Programs, National Institute of Justice, July 1993.

Education Development Center, Inc., Massachusetts Child Exploitation Network. *Child Sexual Exploitation: Improving Investigations and Protecting Victims. A Blueprint for Action.* Washington, DC: U.S. Department of Justice, Office of Justice Programs, Office for Victims of Crime, January 1995.

Fargason CA, Barnes D, Schneider D, Galloway BW. Enhancing multi-agency collaboration in the management of child sexual abuse. *Child Abuse and Neglect* 18(10):859–869, October 1994.

Gable M. Save the children. *UCLA Magazine* 8(1):38–43, June 1996.

Helfer ME, Kempe RS, Krugman RD (eds). *The Battered Child.* 5th ed. Chicago, IL: The University of Chicago Press, 1997.

Henry J. System intervention trauma to child sexual abuse victims following disclosure. *Journal of Interpersonal Violence* 12:4, August 1997.

Jensen JM, Jacobson M, Unrau Y, Robinson RL. Intervention for victims of child sexual abuse: An evaluation of the children's advocacy model. *Child and Adolescent Social Work Journal* 13(2):139–156, April 1996.

Joint investigation: A multidisciplinary approach. *Virginia Child Protection Newsletter* 44:1, 3–7, 16, Winter 1994.

Lanning KV, Walsh B. Criminal investigation of suspected child abuse. In Briere JN et al. (eds): *The APSAC Handbook on Child Maltreatment*. Thousand Oaks, CA: Sage Publications, Inc., 1996.

Lundy JL. *Teams: How to Develop Peak Performance Teams for World Class Results*. Chicago, IL: The Dartnell Corporation, 1992.

MacFarlane K (ed). *MDIT Handbook: A Guide to the Establishment of Multidisciplinary Interview Centers for the Investigation of Child Sexual Abuse*. San Jose, CA: Children's Institute International and Giarretto Institute, 1995.

Marx SP. Victim recantation in child sexual abuse cases: The prosecutor's role in prevention. *Child Welfare* 75(3):219–233, May–June 1996.

Maslach C, Leiter MP. *The Truth About Burnout*. San Francisco, CA: Jossey-Bass Publishers, 1997.

McIntosh-Fletcher D. *Teaming by Design: Real Teams for Real People*. Chicago, IL: Irwin Professional Publishing, 1996.

Missouri State Department of Social Services. *Child Sexual Abuse Protocols*. Jefferson City, MO: Missouri State Department of Social Services, July 8, 1993.

Neb. Rev. Stat. Sec. 28–730 (1997).

New York State Temporary Commission of Investigation. *Secrets That Can Kill: Child Abuse Investigations in New York State*. (Technical Report.) December 1995–January 1996.

Pence D, Wilson C. *Team Investigation of Child Sexual Abuse: The Uneasy Alliance*. (Interpersonal Violence: The Practice Series.) Thousand Oaks, CA: Sage Publications, Inc., 1994.

Phipps CA, Schaefer K, Ventrell MR (eds). Status and trends in child maltreatment laws: Criminal statutes. In *Children's Law,*

Policy and Practice. (Children's Law Manual Series.) Denver, CO: National Association of Counsel for Children, 1995.

Schaufeli W et al. (eds). *Professional Burnout.* Washington, DC: Taylor & Francis, 1993.

Sheppard DI, Zangrillo PA. Coordinating investigations of child abuse. *Public Welfare*, Winter 1996.

Smith BE. *Prosecuting Child Physical Abuse Cases: A Case Study in San Diego.* (NIJ Research in Brief.) Washington, DC: U.S. Department of Justice, Office of Justice Programs, National Institute of Justice, June 1995.

Tjaden PG, Anhalt J. *The Impact of Joint Law Enforcement— Child Protective Services Investigations in Child Maltreatment Cases.* Denver, CO: Center for Policy Research, September 1994.

U.S. Congress. Child Abuse Prevention and Treatment Act of 1974, 42 USC Sec. 5101 et seq., 1997 amendments.

Van Biema D. Abandoned to her fate. *Time Magazine* 146(24), December 11, 1995.

Walsh B. The role of law enforcement in fatal child abuse cases. *APSAC Advisor* 7(4):25–28, Winter 1994.

Organizations

American Professional Society on the Abuse of Children
407 South Dearborn Street, Suite 1300
Chicago, IL 60605
312–554–0166
312–554–0919 (fax)
Internet: www.apsac.org

The American Professional Society on the Abuse of Children (APSAC) is the Nation's only interdisciplinary society for professionals working in the field of child abuse and neglect. It supports research, education, and advocacy that enhance efforts to respond to abused children, those who abuse them, and the conditions associated with their abuse. APSAC's major goal is to promote effective interdisciplinary coordination among professionals who respond to child maltreatment.

Missing and Exploited Children's Training and
  Technical Assistance Program
Fox Valley Technical College
Criminal Justice Department
P.O. Box 2277
1825 North Bluemound Drive
Appleton, WI 54913–2277
800–648–4966
920–735–4757 (fax)
Internet: www.foxvalley.tec.wi.us/ojjdp

The Missing and Exploited Children's Training Program, sponsored by the Office of Juvenile Justice and Delinquency Prevention (OJJDP) and Fox Valley Technical College, offer a variety of courses on investigating child abuse, including an intensive special training for local investigative teams. Teams must include representatives from law enforcement, prosecution, social services, and (optionally) the medical field. Participants take part in hands-on team activity involving:

♦ Development of interagency processes and protocols for enhanced enforcement, prevention, and intervention in child abuse cases.

♦ Case preparation and prosecution.

♦ Development of the team's own interagency implementation plan for improved investigation of child abuse.

National Center for Prosecution of Child Abuse
American Prosecutors Research Institute (APRI)
99 Canal Center Plaza, Suite 510
Alexandria, VA 22314 703–739–
0321
703–549–6259 (fax)
Internet: www.ndaa.org

The National Center for Prosecution of Child Abuse is a nonprofit and technical assistance affiliate of APRI. In addition to research and technical assistance, the Center provides extensive training on the investigation and prosecution of child abuse and child deaths. The national trainings include timely information presented by a variety of professionals experienced in the medical, legal, and investigative aspects of child abuse.

National Clearinghouse on Child Abuse and
  Neglect Information (NCCAN)
330 C Street NW.
Washington, DC 20447 800–
FYI–3366
703–385–7565
703–385–3206 (fax)
Internet: www.calib.com/nccanch

NCCAN provides access to the most extensive, up-to-date collection of
information on child abuse and neglect in the world. The Clearinghouse will
provide, on request, annotated bibliographies on specific topics or a copy of
its data base on CD–ROM. NCCAN also publishes the User Manual
Series, which includes several titles related to MDT's: *A Coordinated Response
to Child Abuse and Neglect: A Basic Manual* (1992), *The Role of Law Enforcement
in the Response to Child Abuse and Neglect* (1992), and *Joint Investigations of Child
Abuse: Report of a Symposium* (1993). These publications are available from
NCCAN.

National Children's Alliance
1319 F Street NW., Suite 1001
Washington, DC 20004–1106
800–239–9950 or
202–639–0597
202–639–0511 (fax)
Internet: www.nca-online.org

Regional Children's Advocacy Centers (CAC's):

♦ Midwest Regional Children's Advocacy Center, St. Paul, MN,
  888–422–2955, 651–220–6750, www.nca-online.org/mrcac.

♦ Northeast Regional Children's Advocacy Center, Philadelphia,
  PA, 215–387–9500, www.nca-online.org/nrcac.

♦ Southern Regional Children's Advocacy Center, Rainbow City, AL,
  256–413–3158, www.nca-online.org/srcac.

♦ Western Regional Children's Advocacy Center, Pueblo, CO,
  719–543–0380, www.nca-online.org/wrcac.

O JJ DP funds the National Children's Alliance and the four regional
CAC's to help communities establish and strengthen CAC and MDT
programs. The Alliance does this by promoting national standard s for
CAC's and providing leadership and advocacy for these programs on a
national level. The Alliance also conducts national training events and
provides grants for CAC program development and support. The four
regional CAC's provide information, onsite consultation, and intensive
training and technical assistance to help establish and strengthen CAC's
and facilitate and support coordination among agencies responding to
child abuse. The Alliance publishes a number of manuals and handbooks
of use to MDT's, including *Handbook on Intake and Forensic Interviewing in
the CAC Setting, Guidelines for Hospital-Collaborative Forensic Investigations of*

Sexually Abused Children, Organizational Development for Children's Advocacy Centers, and *Best Practices.*

National Resource Center on Child Maltreatment (NRCCM)
1349 West Peachtree Street NE., Suite 900
Atlanta, GA 30309
404–876–1934
404–876–7949 (fax)
Internet: www.gocwi.org/nrccm/

NRCCM's objectives are to identify, develop, and promote the application of child protective service models that are responsive to State, tribal, and community needs. Operated jointly by the Child Welfare Institute and ACTION for Child Protection, NRCCM offers training, technical assistance, consultation, and information in response to identified needs relating to the prevention, identification, intervention, and treatment of child abuse and neglect.

Other Titles in This Series

Currently there are 12 other Portable Guides to Investigating Child Abuse. To obtain a copy of any of the guides listed below (in order of publication), contact the Office of Juvenile Justice and Delinquency Prevention's Juvenile Justice Clearinghouse by telephone at 800–638–8736 or e-mail at puborder@ncjrs.org.

Recognizing When a Child's Injury or Illness Is Caused by Abuse, NCJ 160938

Sexually Transmitted Diseases and Child Sexual Abuse, NCJ 160940

Photodocumentation in the Investigation of Child Abuse, NCJ 160939

Diagnostic Imaging of Child Abuse, NCJ 161235

Battered Child Syndrome: Investigating Physical Abuse and Homicide, NCJ 161406

Interviewing Child Witnesses and Victims of Sexual Abuse, NCJ 161623

Child Neglect and Munchausen Syndrome by Proxy, NCJ 161841

Criminal Investigation of Child Sexual Abuse, NCJ 162426

Burn Injuries in Child Abuse, NCJ 162424

Law Enforcement Response to Child Abuse, NCJ 162425

Understanding and Investigating Child Sexual Exploitation, NCJ 162427

Use of Computers in the Sexual Exploitation of Children, NCJ 170021

Notes

Additional Resources

American Bar Association (ABA)
Center on Children and the Law
Washington, DC 202–662–1720
202–662–1755 (fax)

American Humane Association
Englewood, Colorado 800–227–4645
303–792–9900
303–792–5333 (fax)

American Medical Association (AMA)
Department of Mental Health
Chicago, Illinois 312–464–5066
312–464–5000
(AMA main number) 312–464–4184 (fax)

American Professional Society on the Abuse of Children (APSAC)
Chicago, Illinois 312–554–0166
312–554–0919 (fax)

C. Henry Kempe National Center for the Prevention and Treatment of Child Abuse and Neglect
Denver, Colorado 303–864–5250
303–864–5179 (fax)

Federal Bureau of Investigation (FBI)
National Center for the Analysis of Violent Crime
Quantico, Virginia 703–632–4400

Fox Valley Technical College
Criminal Justice Department
Appleton, Wisconsin 800–648–4966
920–735–4757 (fax)

Juvenile Justice Clearinghouse (JJ C)
Rockville, Maryland 800–638–8736
301–519–5212 (fax)

National Association of Medical Examiners
St. Louis, Missouri 314–577–8298
314–268–5124 (fax)

National Center for Missing and Exploited Children (NCMEC)
Alexandria, Virginia 703–235–3900
703–274–2222 (fax)

National Center for Prosecution of Child Abuse
Alexandria, Virginia 703–739–0321
703–549–6259 (fax)

National Children's Alliance
Washington, DC 800–239–9950
202–639–0597
202–639–0511 (fax)

National Clearinghouse on Child Abuse and Neglect Information
Washington, DC 800–FYI–3366
703–385–7565
703–385–3206 (fax)

National SIDS Resource Center
Vienna, Virginia 703–821–8955, ext. 249
703–821–2098 (fax)

Prevent Child Abuse America
Chicago, Illinois 800–835–2671
312–663–3520
312–939–8962 (fax)

www.ingramcontent.com/pod-product-compliance
Lightning Source LLC
Chambersburg PA
CBHW070800180526
45168CB00004B/1699